Copyright © 2018 Tekkan
Artwork Copyright © 2018

All rights reserved.
First Printing, 2018
ISBN 978-1-7324107-5-6

To contact Tekkan please email:
buddhaboy1289@gmail.com

Table of Contents

Galveston. . . . . Page 99

How to Read My Poems

I have married the sonnet to the tanka. I tell a story in the sonnet — using three quatrains, separated by line spaces, and a final couplet. The story builds to a conclusion in the couplet. The tanka is a commentary, or a counterpoint, to the sonnet — the combined poems have two endings.

I don't rhyme my sonnets, because I want freer expression. I want to be direct in my meaning — I want people to clearly understand my meaning. The metaphors are inspired by Shakespeare, and the (aimed-for) precision is in imitation of Japanese style. Using the sonnet with the tanka, I am mixing the sensibility of the Occident and the Orient — which I have done by living in England, Japan, and America.

I don't punctuate much in my poetry. I want the words themselves to do the work. There is logic between words, and the forms provide structure. By not using punctuation I hope to direct readers to carefully attend to each word — to appreciate the graininess of words.

Reading my poems silently, say, on a bus, a train, or an airplane, and reading them aloud, may be different experiences. The way I've written there's not always a pause intended at the end of the line. Hint: *My poems are to be recited not as lines, but as phrases, and a phrase often overflows the break at the end of a line. I pause and take a breath where it seems natural for me to pause. Another person may pause differently than I do.*

Each single poem is a piece of a mosaic, and it is my hope that the collection of poems form an accurate portrait of consciousness.

My daughter, Jocelyn MacDonald, is a wonderful artist. Her art work graces this book.

I am Barry MacDonald. I received the *dharma* name, *Tekkan*, which means, Iron Man, a settled practitioner of great determination.

— *Tekkan*

Everyday Mind VI

Crumpled leaves are
accumulating
on the ground but
my cottonwood is
holding to the last.

Cold Mountain was a Chinese poet who
Wrote his poems on rocks and walls who lived
In a cave within hiking distance of
A Zen temple and people remembered

Him for over a thousand years because
His words are testimony of a life
Given to clouds and mountains and streams and
Meditation as he turned away from

Ordinary frustrations — and we don't
Know whether persecution or failure
Moved him to abandon society
But he cultivated his detachment

To surrender what he had left behind
And to savor the wind passing in pines.

He lingered over
the imperial consorts
of the capital
remembering beautiful
girls enfolded in brocade.

I'm not liberated like Cold Mountain
I haven't left society behind
My wife did leave me but then she returned
We aren't married but nothing else has changed

And I'm still publishing a journal of
Political opinion attending
To bitter controversies without end
As a partisan for liberty so

Half my time is devoted to a cause
And then I'm chasing enlightenment too
Which causes me nothing but frustration
So I am one mixed up *bodhisattva*

Is it necessary to abandon
Society and become a hermit?

My post office box
is my *dana* bowl
everyday I
depend on
donations.

During the hours of a day I am
Capable of being different people
As I appreciate waking up and
Allowing my thoughts to bubble and pop

And when I assume the lotus posture
I generate vigorous energy
So mornings are filled with optimism
And watching the sunrise is glorious

But by afternoon my vibrancy goes
As I dwell on the flow of money or
I get entangled in my opinions
And if difficulties become puzzles

It's possible to question everything
About my yesterdays and tomorrows.

I gain direction
from the might of morning
optimism and
practice circumspection and
tenacity later on.

Words on paper have no meaning if they
Are folded together in a book and
Gathering dust on a shelf even if
They are famous words that everyone could

Recite because communication needs
To be fresh as if you were giving me
A gift and I were holding it in my
Hands and nothing were more important at

The moment — because words are capable
Of resonance across time and space if
I absorb them with my being — because some
Words are authentic and are founded

On experience — and it's possible
I could awaken and live differently.

I am always here
though I am often
dividing myself
by doing two things
at the same time.

When I see half the leaves are on the ground
And the trees are gold red and yellow when
I see the white birch in its glorious
Yellow I want the season to stop and

Linger while the air is mild if only
For a week but I suppose that's the point
Of poignancy — there is no standing still —
There are only consecutive thresholds

And not everyone is present — but even
As I mark the turning year by raking
And bagging leaves even as I engage
In exhilarating activity

I can savor my wholehearted effort
And forget myself doing simple chores.

I pretend every
leaf is a lifetime
of experience
of best intentions
of transitions.

Larry is not conventional and he
Said he has twenty-eight knuckles in his
Hands and the same number in his feet so
All together he enjoys fifty-six

And then he said he has mountains in his
Hands which made me ponder my body and
Whether I have a river in my spine
A burning star in my stomach and an

Ocean in my ears and maybe my mind
Contains the entire universe as
Well as the emptiness that the stars are
Expanding into as everything is

Flowing outward after the Big Bang and
Maybe I'm a particle and a wave.

Dimensions of
reality
flow into me
but can I choose
what's coming out?

I could drift away with the clouds and get
Nothing done and it's easy to think of
Sailors in clippers who relied on block
And tackle on rope and sails to catch the

Wind or to think of farmers on tractors
Plowing their fields who spend lifetimes
Exposed to the sky who labor under
The mixture of light and shadow — but there

Is nothing to grasp and everything is
Fleeting — even though people attended
Carefully and categorized the types
Of clouds and invented names — just try to

Remember tomorrow how the clouds look
Now — and see if your memory is good.

Cirrus
cumulus
cirrocumulus
cumulonimbus
a halo around the sun.

Money is necessary to maintain
The building and to pay the salaries
At the Clouds in Water Zen Temple so
The board of directors initiates

The spring and autumn fundraising campaigns
And a pitch for donations is part of
Every Sunday service and the temple
Requires careful accounting because

We aren't separate from society and
The message of seeing directly in
To the mind and infusing this instant
With as much poise as possible so that

Whatever I do I'm appropriate
Needs a foundation of dollars and cents.

I presume the
frustrations of
earning a living
are included in
everyday *Dharma*.

The Plymouth Voyager

If sentimentality is a sin
I don't care — in remembering how Dad
Was learning not to drive anymore by
Smashing this van through the garage wall twice

In remembering the many times that
Joshua failed his driving tests and how
Inheriting this mangled van was his
Reward for success — in remembering

The many years I drove this Voyager
To Oakaboji and Spirit Lake in
Iowa with my parents my wife and
Kids for our annual vacation so

The natural ending of the van by
Corrosion is a cause for remembrance.

The familiar perch
behind the steering wheel is
like a captain's seat
from which I saw the clouds wind
turbines and cornfields pass by.

He was friendly and persuasive saying
The van was made in the year 2000
Which is unfortunate because in the
Next year Plymouth abandoned the faulty

Mitsubishi engine with a better
Motor which was bullet proof and on this
Voyager the components of the tires
Are only steel and not aluminum

Which would have been more valuable and
He chained the front axle and tilted the
Bed of the tow truck hoisted the van with
An irresistible winch and anchored

The van with chains and he said with regrets
He could give me only fifty dollars.

I spent the fifty
dollars on twenty-eight cans
of cat food because
that's the treatment for Johnnie's
urinary obstruction.

I'm happy my daughter Jocelyn and
Son-in-law Eric have relocated
To Stillwater from Philadelphia
Because instantly I have family

And now my refrigerator is full
Of grapes and concentrated grape juice and
Cheese and meat — and dinners left over from
Yesterday that I decide not to eat

Because they don't belong to me — but on
Halloween they carved pumpkins and spread the
Seeds on tinfoil and a baking pan and
Sprinkled on seasoning and poured over

Worchester sauce and roasted them in the
Oven and days later I swallowed them.

Not the doughnuts
not the cheese puffs
make me blink
but the pumpkin seeds
made me a criminal.

Because I'm smaller than most people I
Became a patron of thrifts stores where there
Is an oversupply of small-sized clothes —
And I bought four pairs of snakeskin — and a

Pair of alligator — cowboy boots — and
I have a closet full of silk and wool
Sports jackets — including the brand names like
Versace and Gucci and Harris Tweed —

And I have a rainbow selection of
Imported silk shirts from Asia — I live
In a prosperous community so
I have access to castoff luxury

That costs me practically nothing — but I'm
Stuck with the chore of lugging them around.

Fashionable
things make me
happy until
dissatisfaction
returns.

My daughter and son-in-law Erick are
Frustrated with me because I forget
To shut the lid of the toilet and their
Cat drinks the toilet water and I've been

Doing my best to remember and the
Point of meditating is to awake —
But yesterday I went to the bank to
Withdraw money to pay a handyman

And I divided the money into
An envelope and my wallet and I
Returned home and realized — I forgot
The envelope at the bank — so I raced

Back to the bank in frustration fuming —
And I found the money on the counter.

I can say — see —
I intend to be
good — but I am
trying to tame a
whirl-wind in my head.

I've heard doors slamming for more than thirty
Years and have grown accustomed to angry
Silences in the household and I'm passed
The confusion of assuming guilt that

Doesn't properly belong to me but
It remains difficult to move about
The bad feelings in the home — and the closed
Door serves as a protecting barrier

Between the two of us — that allows me
To see how trapped you are in your little
Room and how your anger that's hard to face
Is really just a façade that covers

Hurt that does not go away — and at heart
Your wounds from childhood are still festering.

I've learned to balance
powerful emotion with
a dispassionate
practice of meditation —
but you won't accept my help.

An empty sky and bare branches on a
Winter morning appeal to me as the
Sun casts itself on a landscape that's been
Drained of so much vibrancy — because the

Walls of homes the white fence and the crumpled
Leaves on the grass are drenched in a yellow
Light imparting a sense of cheerfulness
Even though the air is penetrating

And the trees are frozen in time — life is
Persisting and I enjoy the force of
The wind moving the needles and branches
Of the pine tree battering me about

My face and bare hands — and the trees may sleep —
But I have to keep moving to stay warm.

A blue sky appears
the same in any season
but the bare trees cast
shadows in a yellow light —
on an earth of drab colors.

I see an overcast sky differently
Once the leaves are down and a dusting of
Snow is on the ground and there's already
Ice on the sidewalk as I get to the

Coffee shop to meet my friends as we've
Gathered together for years — the covering
Clouds mark the threshold of winter but I
Also see the clouds are glowing with light —

And the glow is encouraging as we
Are cultivating enthusiasm
With conversation — and David shows me
A photo a man who was one of

Our group ten years ago and I see he
Fell into a hole in my memory.

I didn't forget
purposely but in
remembering
otherwise
he vanished.

The squirrel jumping between the branches
Of the bare trees in the pale morning light
Of November isn't comparing the
Day's temperature with summer — and it

Doesn't measure the quantity of light
As it's going about the business of
Living even as it has to scramble
To stay warm and fed — but now that the leaves

Are down I can see the squirrel easily
And I can absorb the stillness of the
Season and I can feel the weight of the
Arrival of winter again — and it's

Difficult to escape a measuring
Fear — because life is unpredictable.

Intelligence is
a gift and a curse —
as I can control
so much of my life —
but not everything.

When we meditate together I take
The lotus posture with a straight back and
With crossed legs and I become a breathing
Statue and my breath is inaudible

And as the time passes and energy
Builds my mind becomes a bowl burning all
My thoughts away until I can almost
Forget who I am and I become a

Bubble floating in emptiness but then
Sometimes my throat gets itchy or my nose
Begins to tickle and I swallow to
Suppress a cough or I twitch my nose to

To keep from sneezing but whatever I
Do I just can't prevent an explosion.

I don't want to
be disruptive
but I'm prone
to leakage and
eruption.

When I was a student I tried for an
Hour to describe the way the mown grass smells
In the heat of the summer and I searched
For appropriate words and phrases but

Was finally frustrated because I
Didn't know that the best words were
The names of the things themselves because
The names evoke the experience of

Seeing and smelling and absorbing — and
If you've never heard or seen the water
Flowing over rocks in the woods — when the
Leaves are down and the sky is overcast —

There are no words that can imitate the
Experience of a musical creek.

I used to cloister
myself within study rooms
with a desk and chair
with the walls painted grey
waiting for inspiration.

Year after year the branches return to
Bareness and bring recognition that the
Frost on the roofs and the cold are here for
The duration of winter and the breeze

That was gentle on my face is now sharp
And burns and the multiplicity of
Leaves sighing in the wind is replaced with
A howling or with a stillness that makes

Me imagine the earth is spellbound and
So much that was lively is now absent —
And yet as I see the nakedness of
The branches extending in the grey sky

Diminishing to the most delicate
Of twigs I think of my capillaries.

A burning sun
a beating heart
endure
persist.

Once the cold arrives I resort to the
Thick socks and the insulated jacket
That covers my neck with fabric and I
Wear a wool beret and put on my boots

And when I open the door I'm prepared
For the blast — I leave the car running and
Retreat inside to pour coffee into
Two large thermoses — because life without

Coffee would be meaningless — and then I
Have to put on my wool mittens again —
And turn the doorknob and open the car
Door while holding the thermoses all the

While wearing these thick things on my hands that
Minimize my finger dexterity.

I could put down the
thermoses or remove my
mittens but I like
unlocking the office door
in a flourish of bother.

I'm grateful the journal I'm publishing
Is in difficulty and I don't know
If can pay myself — and I'm thankful
My bills are accumulating — and that

Yoshiko's diabetes and cancer
Are a weight on my mind — because I've been
Muddling along without addressing
The fundamentals of my life and now

That complexity and befuddlement
Have come together while I possess the
Energy of a young man I will throw
Away my dispositions that are not

Useful — and I'll harness the urgency —
To discover what can be accomplished.

Because my troubles
are accumulating and
I don't know what to
do — I'll look for direction
from within and from without.

Entering a temple and becoming
A monk was alluring but I had a
Wife and children to provide for — teaching
English to Japanese in Japan was

Unconventional but we thought our kids
Would do better in American schools —
Starting over in America by
Working for my Dad running a printing

Press editing a publication and
Sustaining a campaign for liberty
Energized me but the operation
Is insecure and my family needs

Stability — for most of the day I
Am inspired but I need more money.

Obstacles may be
opportunities
to evaluate
everything I do
and see what's vital.

Propaganda is flying in the air
And circulating the globe even to
The remotest places and people are
Capable of believing anything

If ideas are presented with flair
And people are accustomed to tribal
Allegiances as we search for a group
Within larger groups to create home

And I'm aware of groupings based on race
Or ideology or a sense of
Historical persecution leading
To a mentality primed for fighting —

I sample the membership messages
But it's difficult for me to commit.

I'm searching for
a consciousness
free of bickering
enclosing people
who are like-minded.

When I think about the people who were
Airbrushed from the photographs of Joseph
Stalin because they fell in disfavor
With the Soviet Union I wonder

Whether the brush dispersed a very fine
Spray of paint or whether in fact color
Was brushed over the person erasing
His personage and I am sure that the

Work was meticulous and demanded
Dexterity — and then I think about
The millions of people who disappeared
Who were airbrushed from the earth in brutal

Fashion erasing their existence in
The service of an ideology.

The reality
is people are capable
of such monstrous
evil while professing the
utmost benevolence.

I don't remember what moved me to ask —
And I can't remember the household chore
She was doing and kept doing — after
She answered — but when my mother said that

Everyone dies a vortex entered my
Life — as a black hole was introduced — and
I couldn't understand what it meant that
Everyone grows old and even children

Can disappear and I wondered for the
First time where will I go — that even my
Home and neighborhood and my parents could
Not protect me from the dread of a death —

I don't remember what I was doing —
But I do remember being afraid.

My knowledge
and imagination
bump up against
ignorance and
I also forget.

I've read sailors' tales of a squall on the
Horizon that raises a fury of
Wind and rain when they had to climb and furl
Their sails in a tumultuous ocean

But catching an early winter cold is
Less dramatic and more gradual with
A soreness arising in my back and
Chest with my throat becoming hoarse and my

Head suddenly dizzy — and I have to
Rise from bed and dress laboriously —
And the road I'm driving on doesn't roll
And tumble and the wind isn't howling

But the bare trees and the grey sky are here
And there is no escape in grumbling.

I'm here for the
duration of
the winter — an
able-bodied
Minnesotan.

I welcome myself on my return to
My chair and window and keyboard and screen
Where I watch the world and formulate words
Because it's marvelous to see with a

Clear mind and body liberated from
A cold appreciating energy
Resuming my routines when I notice
How heavy the handle of the coffee

Pot feels as it fills with water and how wide
Apart I place my hands on the steering
Wheel while gliding on the familiar streets
And how my pens and books and papers are

Just where I left them but there's a frosting
On the roofs — remarkable this morning.

I can turn my head
without discomfort
following a hawk
gliding under a
white sky.

There's not a straight line in the cottonwood
Not even one elegant curve as it
Stands revealed in the frosty air of
The morning a dangling monstrosity

Of crooks and crags far too numerous and
Much too irregular to remember —
And even though it's by my house where I've
Lived for twenty years it's impossible

To describe in detail except to say
Its trunk is wide — and it towers over
Every other tree — and it's roots broke my
Sewage pipe — but if I closed my eyes I

Couldn't accurately imagine its
Form because there's nothing to grasp hold of.

I see two large crows
alighting on the highest
branches opposite
each other establishing
a cottonwood battlement.

I admire guys with hairy faces
Who grow hair evenly without the gaps
Most men have who from the first day that they
Stop shaving and every morning when they

Look in the mirror can see a steady march
To masculine satisfaction — but for
Me I stagger through desolate days of
Scruffiness when I know I look awful

But I think of my cottonwood as a
Paragon of nature because there is
No symmetry and every inch and curve
And twig is uniquely twisted and that's

OK — so I stay away from mirrors
Until my beard becomes presentable.

It's been years since I've
started and I'm doing it
only because change
is intriguing — I want to
see how a white beard will look.

Winter is the time for watching squirrels
Because they are exposed in bare branches
And I can see them clamber up and chase
Each other while nothing else is moving

And sunrises are spectacular in
Winter because they light an otherwise
Bleak landscape with ruby and violet
And orange and yellow and winter is

A season for meditation when I
Can see through the naked trees and the air
Is crisp and the sound of a car on a
Street reverberates and I can use the

Clarity and the tranquility of
Winter to question what is important.

Nothing is idle
and everything is moving
according to its
nature but I can pause and
consider where I'm going.

There is a bubble of peace about me
Because I work alone in a quiet
Neighborhood where I can watch the sun rise
Every morning but a point comes in the

Day when I turn my attention to the
News and lately women are accusing
Famous and powerful men of abuse
And the everyday fascination with

Victims and villains and recrimination
Is consuming new personalities
And while there are victims and villains
And recrimination can be useful

The news is always a stew of gossip
Excited by daily accusation.

I am a human
animal susceptible
as people are to
the cauldron of gossip but
I know it's dispiriting.

The monks at *Hosshinji* in Japan shave
Their heads as Buddhists monks have always done
For more than a thousand years because they
Want to sever attachment to worldly

Concerns as they know hair is easy to
Admire — and that's also why the Zen Priests
Wear mostly black robes with a splash of brown
To signify the highest status — and

The graininess of the wooden *Zendo*
Where everyone meditates is left a
Natural brown that's easy to forget
In the quest for enlightenment so that's

Why the tall monk Daigaku took offense
When I ambled about in a blue scarf.

Disapprovingly
he approached to take
my scarf and tuck it
in my black sweatshirt
re-establishing peace.

I was a bit lackadaisical in
The rigor I was determined to use
In my practice of Zen detachment from
Worldly affairs and ten years ago

When I was making more money than now
I bought two large rings of the same design —
Of a roaring lion with a mane in
The shape of a circle surrounding his

Face — and the gold ring has a diamond mouth
And diamond eyes — and the silver ring has
An open mouth and eyes — and I used to
Wear the rings on my middle fingers but

Now they are an impediment to my
Typing and I seldom want to wear them.

The bulky rings
made typing
difficult so
I returned to
simplicity.

Once I know the impetus of anger
And experience the raw energy
Coming with a seething resentment that
Makes me a superman for a few hours

I realize a threshold is crossed — and
Afterwards I am exhausted and left
With an altered mentality with a
Poisoned point of view so difficult to

Escape — but once I experiment and
Speak kindly and behave gently I don't
Need my justifications and my gloom
Dissipates and forgiveness is easy —

I'm not grasping for enlightenment but
I do appreciate a quiet head.

So much anger
is floating about
society but
running away is
not a solution.

It comes in the windows and even through
The walls the minute the furnace takes a
Break from heating the home as we have drawn
The curtains and locked the doors but there is

No mitigation of the weight of the
Cold on a winter night in December
In Minnesota even though we passed
The solstice and daylight will get longer

Gradually we face the coldest days
Of the year so it's not just tonight that
Is bearing down it's the burden of our
Knowledge of the months coming and there is

No use in grumbling so I put on my
Thick socks and pile up the heavy blankets.

While walking around
during the daylight only
a little oval
including my mouth eyes and
nose is exposed to the cold.

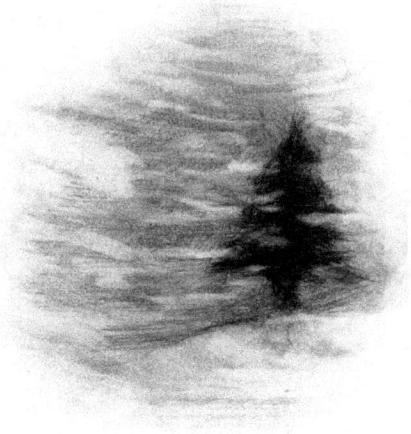

Kit Cat knows where to go in the house to
Take advantage of circumstances and
Yesterday during the coldest day of
The year he was dozing on the fuzzy

Blanket on my bed in a morning beam
Of sunlight dreaming Kit Cat dreams and this
Afternoon he was on his back stretching
His front and back legs happily in front

Of the vent that channels the heat from the
Furnace into the bathroom that is the
Smallest and so is also the warmest
Room in the house and he rolled upon a

Comfy mat when he saw me and closed his
Eyes saying — look how I am relaxing.

He doesn't have to
shovel snow today
doesn't confront
the biting cold doesn't wield
a shovel and snow blower.

Kit Cat doesn't bother controlling his
Tail and it follows mindlessly but when
Sitting pertly he curls it around from
The right and when he is watching me

In a crouch while I'm washing the dishes
Sometimes the tip of his tail will flick to
The right and left and in the morning when it's
Time for brushing his tail goes up as he lopes

Away and sometimes I see him poised to
Pounce and his tail is tense and when he is
Wrestling with the other cats Johnny
Or Henry there isn't any grace as

His tail is whipping in a furious
Chaos unpredictable and jerky.

I don't detect a
reflection of
sophistication or
commiseration
in his tail.

I would have to be careful if I had
A long tail because it would give away
My secrets and if I were impatient
I'd be snapping it back and forth and if

Angry my hair would stand up and my tail
Would be stiff behind me and if I were
Afraid I would not dangle but I would
Look angry — yet if I were embarrassed

Or disconsolate I would droop — and if
Curious or excited there would be
Swishing and swinging and if perplexed I
Think it would be frozen but with people

Watching me I wouldn't think about it —
I would assume a jaunty confidence.

While sitting
in a chair I would
swing my tail around
from the left because
I am left-sided.

My knowledge of science informs me that
The oxygen molecules closest to
The candlewick are moving faster than
Molecules further off and the result

Is the candlelight in the dark — and the
Christmas tree is electrically lighted
And I am enjoying the Christmas tree
And the presents and the candle light and

I am remembering everything that
Happened in this tricky and exhausting
Year — the weariness and satisfaction —
And I think it is extraordinary

That such an elementary thing as
Combustion can inspire emotion.

Somehow particles
elements and molecules
create seasons and
families and
Christmas.

The below zero cold has a way of
Waking me up in the morning that is
More impactful than a fender bender
While driving on the slippery roads of

Stillwater but as I bundle up and
Protect my feet and hands and ears I am
Almost impervious to the hostile
Air as I'm stomping about the snow in

My boots — but it's the inconvenience of
Putting on and taking off everything
Day after day that gets to me as the
Chore is unavoidable unless I

Don't care a bit about leaving puddles
Of melted snow from my boots behind me.

Unlocking doors while
wearing mittens and
holding containers
of coffee is an
everyday chore.

After leaving the conversation at
The coffee shop after our Saturday
Morning meditation I intended
To write poetry but realized that

My cell phone was missing so I searched the
Office with no relief and rushed back to
The Zendo where I used it to keep time
But it wasn't there so I returned to

The coffee shop hoping to seize it with
No luck and on the way back to my desk
I remembered the phone was more than a
Year old and I could buy a new one for

Twenty dollars a month over two years
But there it was being charged on a book.

The whirlwind had
returned to my
head as I forgot
to do one thing
at one time.

New Year's Day

It is worth recognizing — worth overdoing —
The holiday celebration with the
Dropping ball in New York City and the
Fireworks in Sydney Australia though

From one point of view it's just another
Second minute hour day week and year
Parceled out as long as anyone cares
To notice — the frictionless motion of

The earth and moon goes on unconsciously —
But for us the sun appears to rise and
Set and for me it's helpful to muster
My energy in bursts of effort that

I can measure with segments of time so
I can focus on accomplishments.

The cold
is impossible to
ignore but I will
attend to what I am
doing now.

I have struggled and competed enough
And I have compared myself with others
And I don't know how to stop measuring
Myself — and feeling the ups and downs of

Competition — and so the Buddha's words
Are alluring and I am practicing
To forget myself and to monitor
The subtle tricks I use to reinforce

Identity but I also love to
Play with words and harmonize rhythm and
Meaning and I enjoy discovering
How much reality I can capture —

There are moments of spontaneous joy
When words and ideas come together.

The master said
awakening happens
instantaneously —
do one thing
at one time.

I was driving through Stillwater doing
A chore turning on familiar streets and
I noticed the sun appearing with a
Right turn and with a left turn there was

The early morning moon — and I was in my
Working mind following the streets and the
Turns of the city but the sun and moon
Kept popping up around a corner and

Seemed to follow me — the moon was looming
White but yesterday it was yellow in
The dark — and there in a window was the
Lively reflection of the sun shining

Gold and my eyes didn't hurt in lingering
Over the sight — and then I was driving.

The sun and moon are
unearthly beauty
everyone can see —
they enliven the
sky everyday.

There are a hundred things more important
Today and after sixty years of life
I know how to leverage my energy
To achieve the most productivity

But it's one of the indignities of
Living to discover when pulling on
My wool sock that a cuticle has grown
At the base of the nail of my little

Toe and it's irritating to feel the
Growth standing up and catching on the wool —
And until it's gone it will be like a
Stone in my shoe so I am going to scrunch

Myself to reach the toe with clippers and
Angle in carefully and cut it out.

In the scheme of life
I wonder what is
the purpose of a
cuticle that grows
on a little toe.

Kit Cat often jumps to the countertop
In the kitchen even though we push him
Off and scold him — he is determined and
Perhaps he feels dominant when he takes

A high position — and one day I was
Sitting on the couch in the living
Room within sight of the countertop watching
The television and Kit Cat knocked a

Container off the countertop and I
Heard it plop and saw him looking at me
Waiting for me to respond and I knew
He was manipulating me so I

Made of show of opening and closing
The drawers and I even turned a doorknob.

He stretched up
to move the knob
with his paws but
couldn't and I
said nothing.

Kit Cat is not like Johnnie and Henry
Who want me to brush them and when I sit
On the floor and call they come and Jonnie
Will even turn around for me to brush

The other side while Kit is watching from
A distance because he knows he's next and
From experience he knows if he hides
Behind the T.V. I'll grab him later

But he runs to make me chase and then I
Kneel with him before me and brush while he
Complains and afterwards he struts away —
But one day he seized the brush from my hands

And holding it with his front paws he nailed
It with his back paws and then scampered off.

Kit determines
how to respond —
he will not be
a docile follower.

To be awake and spontaneous in
A way that does not summon negative
Consequences I have to acquire
Optimism and persistence and I

Need to have transcended the grip of fear
That can so easily infect every
Aspect of my personality — as
I have learned it's useless to run from my fears —

It's better to recognize my fears and
Do what's necessary and base my faith
On the assumption that I am living
A life that never ends but does transform —

So whatever impediments arise
Before me are only ephemeral.

It's necessary
for me to transcend my fears
and to base my faith
on a persisting goodness
I can grow into.

So what does my spontaneity do
When a cold front is coming in behind
The falling snow with the expectation
Of the return of below zero cold

With my long underwear washed and ready
With my cold weather boots and mittens and
A hood attached to my jacket that makes
Me mostly invulnerable to the

Weather as I'm absorbing the gloomy
Sky and the bare branches and the drizzle
That will become a dump of heavy wet
Snow that I will be removing soon — how

Does spontaneity show itself on
A day when everyone just wants to hide?

I go about the
day as buoyant as if it
were a cloudless day
in summer realizing
the sun does make the clouds glow.

There is a saying that sticks in my mind
About a Zen master who asserts that
People he meets are not different people —
They are himself — and I'm not sure of his

Meaning and I can't quite make the jump in
Understanding to see as he does but
I often catch myself watching my friends
And acquaintances and my family

And I gauge their reactions to me as
If they were mirrors reflecting on my
Worthiness and even though I know what
I'm doing sometimes it's difficult to

Escape the weight of self-obsession so
I will put my faith in transformation.

Zen masters use
riddles that stick
in the mind like
a returning
itch.

When Zen people get together we like
To ring a bell to signify when it's
Time to enter the Zendo and begin
Our meditation and some people get

The urge to hit the bell for no reason
Except to hear it ring but as the guy
In charge I frown on unsanctioned ringing
So when Jane casually moved to strike

The bell I came behind her back and with
Her stroke I immediately pinched the
Bell and re-established the quiet — but
I failed to anticipate what Jane would

Do standing with a mallet in her hand
And she hit me — a thunk — on my forehead.

It is fortunate
I am not the guy in charge
of military
strategy as I fail to
think of probabilities.

If I were an angel liberated
From the disagreements and frustrations
Of everyday living there would be no
Possibility for growth on the earth

And I wouldn't feel misunderstood and
Separate and I wouldn't doubt myself —
Nor would I question everything — nor would
I experience fear — angels are dreams

Of the imagination and serve as
Emissaries for a goodness that is
Invisible and untouchable so
Often — but I have come to live for those

Days when I do something surprising and
Find satisfaction and liberation.

The things I do
have resonance
informing me of
consequence if I
attend carefully.

When I'm sitting quietly before dawn
There is nothing in the house to distract
Me from myself and that is when I get
To know the acrobatics of my mind

And there is always a choice whether to
Follow the direction of my thoughts and
Whether to become enamored of the
Emotion attached to my thinking or

To let the whirl-wind go and because a
Thought and the emotion connected to
The thought will take a natural amount
Of time as long as I'm not obsessing

I may practice holding up the bowl of
My mind — letting the bowl fill and empty.

I am the
emptiness
the emotion
passes through —
I am watching.

A car is a modern-day chariot
And a symbol of personality
That also serves as armor against the
Extremes of cold and heat and snow and rain

And when ensconced inside I listen to
The radio fascinated with my
Political controversies and when
Bored I turn to music stimulating

Pathways in my brain that make me vibrate
And someone is always driving slower
Than me and I can't pass or someone is
Behind me desperately wanting to get

Around and whatever's happening it's
Difficult to do one thing at one time.

Sometimes I turn
the radio off
and my thinking
is exposed.

January is January when
It gets as cold as it ever does in
Minnesota and doing anything
Outside is complicated like turning

Keys while wearing mittens and holding my
Two containers of coffee in the dark
And it's my fingers and toes and ears that
Need protecting while my nose is OK

But then there is the January thaw
When the snow on the driveway and sidewalk
And on the city roads too smears itself
Onto my boots and car and the sticky

Mess is everywhere and everyone leaves
Behind a trail of salty nastiness.

As a veteran
of winters I use
lotion on my
fingers and Lip Balm
to prevent cracking.

We don't refer to barometers or
Rely on eyewitnesses in the west —
We don't even have to watch the bearing
Of the clouds anymore because we have

Weather people broadcasting satellite
Images but in the morning with my
Group of sober alcoholics I said
The snow was late and everyone was wrong

Because when it snows an icon appears
On my phone of little white dots but now
There are solid black bars clearly meaning
We have escaped the snow again today

And Joe said I could be in denial
But momentarily we will know truth.

Spinning and swerving
I progressed about an inch
and had to shovel
again to clear my tires
because snow was everywhere.

There is no use in grumbling in the
Middle of a storm and I was lucky
To get my car in the garage before
The accumulating snow made driving

Impossible so I zipped on my one
Piece suit and chose the hat with ear flaps and
Tugged on my boots and prepared for battle —
And I pulled snow off the roof with a rake

And set the snow blower at the slowest
Speed and trudged forward spewing a steady
Stream and when the driveway was cleared I took
My shovel and proceeded to stab and

Fling along the walkway and was almost
Finished before my fingers were frozen.

I wear the woolen
mittens from an army
surplus store but
after a while my
fingers always freeze.

As I see the morning light painting the
Cottonwood orange and I notice a
Mountainous pile of snow bordering the
Street along my property things appear

As they should in January after
A snowfall and yet it seems I'm on a
Journey in a world of surprises and
Even though a heavy snowfall often

Happens and the city plows do what they
Always do and every winter I clear
The driveway and shovel the walkway
This morning my familiar neighborhood

Is hidden by a foot of the freshest
Snow under a blue sky showering light.

The lilac bush is
bare — the trees are brown but
my magnificent
cottonwood is reflecting
the glorious sun.

It's convenient to parcel out my life
In days and weeks because the rising and
The setting sun is easy to go by —
And if there weren't day interspersed with night

It would be much harder to remember
What I did last week — and I am really
Grateful for my eyes to see bare branches
In a blue sky and grateful for my skin

And body so I can know what the cold
Of winter is — and also there is my
Marvelous mind that reminds me while a
Chill is rising from the snow on the ground

In several months the roses bloom again
And in summer I may wear a t-shirt.

I see the moon in
the morning and in
the afternoon too —
it's an everyday
presence to go by.

When I understand nothing moves faster
Than light and that the light from distant stars
Traveled billions of years to reach the earth
Then I appreciate immensity

And when I understand that during the
Passage of the light the stars radiating
The light have imploded and no longer
Exist then I encounter mystery —

And when I consider that the forces
Of gravity are whirling galaxies
And everything that exists is moving
In relation to every other thing

Then I have to put my life and efforts
In context with a sobering cosmos.

I have questions
and would like
solutions but
also I love
a rising sun.

The light a star generates radiates
In all directions and on earth we see
The cosmos from a limited point of
View and I believe it's necessary

To question where we are going and to
Grasp purposes worthy of our living
Because we have the curiosity
And the wherewithal to comprehend so

Many of the facts about us and we
Know immensity and minuteness and
We understand our tininess within
The universe but no one can explain

How our molecules and electrical
Impulses create thought and emotion.

The immensity
of the cosmos is nothing
compared with the
everyday miracle of
ordinary consciousness.

I am a seeker of inspiration
And when confused or afraid or angry
I have had to practice patience because
Patience seems the best medicine in the

Middle of disagreement — and sometimes
The best I can do is not to express
All the anger within me but to leave
An argument unresolved and to let

People believe what they want about me
At least until circumstances change and
The unreasonable expectations
Anyone could have are recognized and

Sorted out — even sharp emotions can
Be useful if I can summon patience.

The morning after
an argument I
can cherish
justifications or let
emotions dissipate.

There is no predicting of the rewards
Coming from patient observation once
A time of day is set apart and the
Chattering of distracting thought is tamed

When I come to my desk at the same time
Everyday to find what is worthy of
Remembering today as I see the
Same ground and trees and houses that were here

Yesterday and sometimes disagreements
And angry words reverberate but now
There is a covering of snow and the
Crystals of snow are shining in the light

And the apple tree is slightly frosted
And the far horizon is blue and white.

Some days I don't
see the trees in
front of me
because words are
reverberating.

Some people claim to have mind palaces
Meaning they have the ability to
Store and recall the information they
Use efficiently and perhaps there are

Porticos and vestibules attached to
The ornate chambers of rumination
And maybe when a question arises
There is a salon where the various

Voices of opinion can debate and
I suppose that the most superior
Amble about with a structure much like
A gothic cathedral in their heads

But I struggle when tying my shoe to
Simply tie my shoe without distraction.

I was reversing
in a parking lot
and smacked into a
car that wasn't there
a moment ago.

The earth is turning on its axis and
Revolving about the sun and even
Our solar system is caught in a net
Of gravity so everything is in

Motion — and with my first sip of coffee
In the morning warmth coincides with the
Sunlight and optimism and play with
Words but in the afternoon energy

Dissipates and doubts and fears arise so
Every emotion is transitory —
Everyday I see the same branches of
The same trees and enjoy my rootedness

In this place even as I am gaining
Momentum and moving to mystery.

I protect myself
with repetition
but need to
leave room for
innovation.

A flame of consciousness is consuming
This moment considering everything
Evaluating priorities and
Preparing a response and I know how

Precarious my perceptions are and
How vulnerable I am to waves of
Combustive emotion because there is
A hunger for love and a fear that love

Is unobtainable as my thoughts are
Whispering I am not worthy of love
And I recognize the burning power
And I know such thinking is deluded

And believe many endure such thinking
So I will practice letting go of thought.

I prefer a
candle's radiance
but endure
lusty fire.

Cold Mountain followed the tradition of
The Chinese poets who left the cities
And roamed the country in solitude but
The river and mountain poets wanted

Their poems to be celebrated — Cold
Mountain rejected the snares and misery
And futility of civilized life
And he used the conventions the other

Poets did but he wrote his poems on the
Rocks and walls and trees with no intention
Of preserving them — and only through the
Efforts of others were they saved and passed

Down the centuries to show he was a
Poet who gave himself to expression.

In a dream a
woman with white
hair was looking
at him but did not
recognize him.

I meditate before dawn and meet with
Sober alcoholics for talk and for
Most of the day every day I have a
Clear head and am enthusiastic and

I practice composing words into lines
And search for appropriate words in good
Order and sometimes it's necessary
To start over again and sometimes I

Have to wait for a word to arise and
When it does it is recognizable
As a word worth waiting for on the way
To a couplet epitomizing a

Sonnet in which every word is correct
And the sonnet reveals simplicity.

The word arising
is a rediscovery
of what I already
knew but hadn't
yet signified.

The iron in my body came from an
Exploding star billions of years ago
And my body is composed of atoms
And molecules and strands of DNA

That testify to an origin I
Share with every living being on earth
And within my body there are layers
Of organization where cells behave

Independently and for the good of
The whole also so that I can sit at
My table and cut an orange into
Pieces and taste the taste of an orange

And I can speculate from this table this
Moment is moving to infinity.

There are billions
and billions of stars
in space and atoms
in my body — there is
also consciousness.

Scientists uphold a prism of glass to
Separate the light into colors and
They aim spectroscopes to see the colors
Of starlight and thereby they deduce the

The age and chemical composition
Of the most distant stars and in a few
Thousand years by working together they
Have exposed the swirling cosmos and the

Inescapable fragility of
Humanity too and yet our human
Comprehension resembles a super
Nova bursting and seeding the empty

Spaces with a consciousness that will not
Be satisfied with lingering questions.

Even before the
questions could be
formulated there was
cooperation — there were
words.

Drunks with my genetic disposition
Usually don't live to reach my age
But if they do they leave behind a trail
Of misery and misunderstanding

And recrimination because until
An alcoholic or a drug addict
Surrenders and embodies a power
Greater than himself and until he is

Reformed by invisible power and
Is encouraged by everyday friendship
With fellow alcoholics who are on
The same path the addict is a whirlwind

Because he and his family do not
Understand — he's lost control of himself.

Perhaps one in ten
can't stop consuming
drugs or alcohol
but there is power
and recovery.

A drunk's thinking is all mixed up and his
Whirling thoughts cannot be separated
From the urge to drink and by himself he
Is confounded — though he is blind to his

Predicament and sincerely believes
He is a victim of circumstances —
There is a powerful charge attached to
Thinking and emotion and a drunk is

Lost in suppositions while the drink used
To bring sanctuary and pleasure but
As alcoholism progresses the
Respite from misery vanishes and

There is no escape from isolation
And he slowly begins to hate himself.

Why doesn't he change
his attitude and reform
himself — is it so
difficult not to take the
first drink?

The descent into the desperation
Of alcoholic thinking comports with
The poison of alcohol but once the
Drunk has surrendered and becomes willing

To do anything for sobriety
She enters into the circles of light
Hearted conversation where she will find
Companions who share her experience

And she will be offered a process of
Recovery that cuts across the grain
Of ordinary self-reliance and
Points to an unspecified power of

Her interpretation that already
Exists but has been inaccessible.

Dead end
behavior is
exhausted and
new thinking is
possible.

The immensities of the cosmos and
The impersonality of the laws
Of physics don't matter that much to me
Nor do I care that for most of human

Experience there was no remedy
For the curse of alcoholism — the
Fact is I have been sober for more
Than thirty years by cultivating a

Faith in a power greater than myself
A power I am growing into based
On love and forgiveness and gratitude
And I believe whatever happens to

Me I will be OK even if I
Die because consciousness will persevere.

The cosmos may
expand forever with
dark mass and
dark energy
nobody understands.

The ancient Chinese were meticulous
But they lacked our accumulation of
Knowledge so they could not understand the
Behavior of an atom but the words

Of Zen monks transmitted through centuries
Testify that the rocks and grasses and
Mountains are moved by an unborn and an
Undying presence in everything that

Does not hurry and yet accomplishes
The sowing and the harvesting of the
Seasons in proper time and the river
And mountain poets of China aspired

To harmonize their passions with the cloud
Generating mountains and with the moon.

They cultivated
unflinching poise
uncompromising
receptivity
to whatever comes.

Can you see the questing spirit in the
River and mountain poets and in the
Solitary living of Cold Mountain
Exploring the wilderness of China?

They were the mandarins and keepers of
Tradition who became dissatisfied
With the exercise of power and who
Wanted to pursue the mysterious

Allure of nature by leaving cities
And experimenting with their bodies
With sensations and consciousness watching
And learning from the seasons attending

To the emergence and disappearance
Hearing the gibbons howling in the trees.

They applied
consciousness
and experience
distilling nature
in everyday mind.

I enjoy learning about the quirks and
Quarks of space/time but there was a foot of
Snow last night and I was too leisurely
About its removal from my driveway

And when I aroused myself the sun was
Beaming and the moist snow was clogging my
Snow blower and the realization
Came it was necessary to shovel

The imposing pile the city plow had
Left blocking my entrance and I had to
Slice the snow with the side of my shovel
To loosen it and then I had to make

A wide base to heap a mountain of snow
Upon at both corners of the driveway.

Snow accumulates
during the winter and can
only be piled to
a certain height and so
the mountains grow sideways.

It wasn't pleasant to realize I
Had to shovel the entire driveway
Because the snow was too wet and heavy
For the snow blower but my revulsion

Wasn't moving snow so after the pile
At the entrance was hurled to the sides I
Began to push snow with my shovel on
The asphalt and discovered the power

Of my hips and legs and momentum and
I forgot the driveway and walkway by
Just moving the bit of snow here and by
Indulging animal energy and

By pacing and after finishing I
Surveyed my driveway with satisfaction.

The snow continued
to melt but I took
a photo with my
phone to remember
the enormity.

I am taking time to look at the creases
Of my palms and to appreciate the
Many fine wrinkles they have grown into
And there are the insides of my fingers

That I'm flexing and then I turn my wrists
And see the blood vessels on the backs of
My hands and remember in a moment
I did unzip my jacket and hold the

Sides and pull the jacket off without a
Thought about how useful my hands are and
I realize that I constantly do
Hold and grip and pull and twist and turn and

Rub and caress and touch with the tips of
My fingers without appreciation.

The world is as it
is but I wouldn't know so
much if I couldn't
pick it up and hold it and
explore with my fingers.

A boxer has trained to get maximum
Impact into a blow and he imparts
Leverage coming from his legs and hips
And abdomen as force swells throughout his

Body and is focused in several
Knuckles and I believe he has fashioned
His spirit for the giving and taking
Of punishment and has cultivated

A personality for a contest
Of wills with a style of evasion and
Attack and a magic of motion that
Earns him a name and reputation but

I wonder whether the effort precludes
The opening of his gentility.

The warrior
stands on the earth
and the impetus of force
arises from the earth
and flows through his body.

A lover is like everyone and is
Distracted by a thousand details as
He goes about his days rushing to get things
Done but a lover is also awake

And takes the time to feel the grain of the
Wooden chest of drawers and notices the
Texture of the cotton undershirt as
He takes it out and puts it on and knows

Its lightness — and holds the steel container
Of coffee and weighs it in his hand and
Drinks closing his eyes and following the
Warmth going down and spreading out — even

On the busiest day it's possible
To appreciate the world in passing.

A lover's love
emanates from
unreasonable
unexplainable
gratitude.

Writing poetry is a method that
Generates enthusiasm and gets
Me out of bed and even my dreams
Are inspiration for poetry and

Usually I'm happy because of
My poems but there comes a time in the
Day for doing the work that generates
A paycheck by means of publishing a

Journal of political opinion
When I turn from the ethereal and
Become realistic and when I hear
People say regarding their opinions —

I follow my heart — I think we would do
Much better if you were more circumspect.

There is just too
much detail and
deception woven
in the framing of
political words.

When young and ignorant I watched my Dad
Engage in political writing and
Was repulsed by the severity of
His attitude but after observing

How politics is maneuvered it is
Manifest that the most effective ploy
Is to be smugly righteous and accuse
The other guy of inhumanity

And if the accusation is brief and
Easy to digest the facts don't matter
And the news people will cooperate
Because passion creates an audience

And it is propitious if the news
Media and the accuser agree.

Too often
politics is not
about solving
problems.

European revolutionaries
Figured out centuries ago that the
Way to manipulate the masses was
To use the obvious disparity

Common in societies divided
By class and to demonize the King and
The aristocracy and the bishops
And they circulated their pamphlets

On equality and liberty and
On brotherhood but they relied on hate
And violence and whatever good was
Intended was overwhelmed in a rush

Of accusation without mercy and
The usual use of a guillotine.

Revolutions are
made of zealotry
and revenge
not charity
or justice.

There are conspiracies behind doors and
In the corridors of the capital
In the best of times and the secrets and
The trading of influence the public

Doesn't see is justified because the
Conspirators are lawmakers who are
Expert at serving the public interest
With a show of articulate concern

And a wealthy nation has a heap of
Tax revenue to divvy up and a
Pile of regulating to do and the
Tax code is too complicated but it

Benefits the corporations that know
Whom to call and how much to contribute.

An exquisite
system of laws and
a balancing of powers
aren't quite enough
to compel compassion.

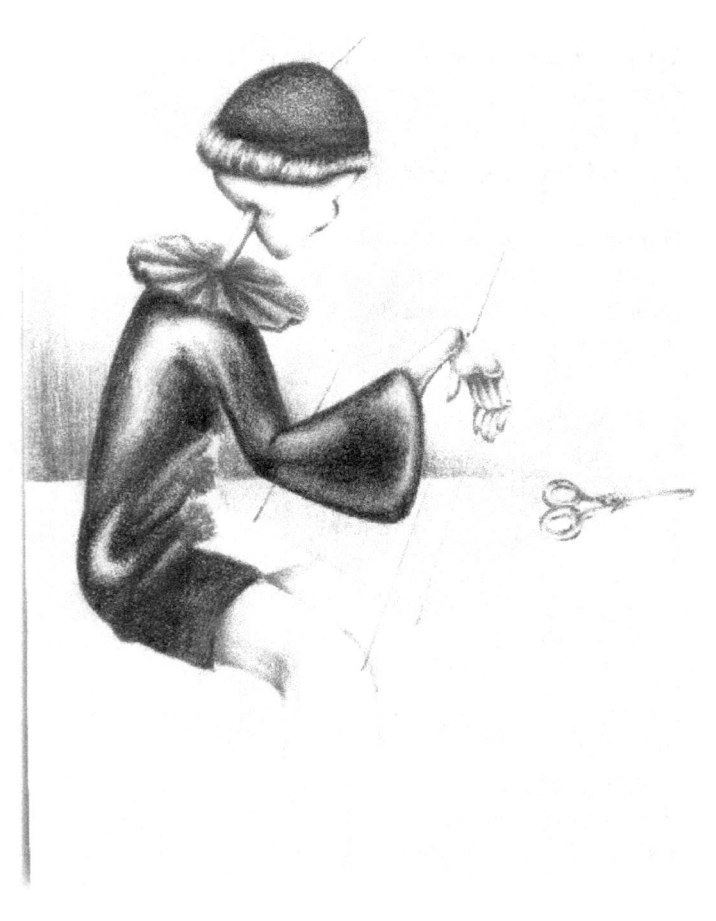

The Washington Correspondents Dinner
Is a black tie affair where the nation's
Top news personalities gather to
Celebrate their prominence because they

Comprehend the complexities at the
Apex of government and they serve as
Mediators for the ignorant and
The downtrodden and they exemplify

The better angels of America's
Conscience as it is necessary to
Remind our nation of historical
Misdeeds and we should have gratitude for

This collection of special intellects
For providing such gentle correction.

They are the
guardians of
democracy and
the library of
the law.

Does anyone remember Walt Whitman
Our loafing poetic American
Hero who discovered the cosmos in
A blade of grass who celebrated the

Exuberance of the nation he loved
A nation of heroes who constructed
The California Aqueduct and the
Empire State Building and the Hoover

Dam and who sent astronauts to the moon
But Walt Whitman also cared for and grieved
For the dismembered and dying soldiers
In our nation's capital during the

Civil War and he memorialized
American tragedy with his words.

Too many
Americans today
are ashamed of
America.

The Internal Revenue Service tried
To extinguish our publication thirty
Years ago by revoking our status
As an educational foundation

Because some small-minded bureaucrat was
Offended by our political point
Of view so they sent an agent with a
Mission to examine our books and my

Dad provided a chair and table in
The garage but he wasn't permitted
Inside the office and the I.R.S.
Failed ignominiously to stop us

When the governor of Minnesota
Responded and compelled them to retreat.

Throughout the
intrusion my Dad
continued to play
golf in the afternoon
at the club.

It is fashionable today to be
Skeptical and even a little bit
Suspicious of explicit displays of
Manliness and there are thinkers at our

Universities proposing that the
Usual views of male and female roles
Are outdated constructs of a worn out
World and we should be excited and be

Liberated with new alternative
Modes of being — and didn't we suspect
While watching the swaggering bravado
Of the clownish cowboy John the Duke Wayne

There was something exaggerated and
More than a little crazy about him?

We don't have to
be oppressed by
testosterone — we
can repudiate
toxic masculinity.

I didn't like my Dad for many years
Because he wasn't in tune with the times
When I was a teenager listening
To rock music and I didn't want to

Be seen with him as he was serious and
Aloof and embarrassing while I was
Dreaming of a separate world full of
Romance without his presence but looking

Back I perceive our home was orderly
And we had the necessities of life
And I believe it's not unusual
To turn away from the imposition

Of authority while at the same time
Relying on the protection he gave.

Now I know
from seeing wreckage
in America
boys are lost
without fathers.

The temperature at the core of the
Sun is ten million degrees and the force
Of gravity is fusing nuclei
Of hydrogen atoms together and

Producing helium and energy —
And it takes ten million years for the heat
And the light to percolate and emerge
At the surface of the sun — and it takes

Only eight minutes to radiate to
The horizon in front of my desk and the
Light illuminates craggy cottonwood
Bark and the light comes through the window and

Through my eyes into the synapses of
My brain empowering my consciousness.

The sun on my cheeks
originated ten million
years ago in the
core of the sun ninety
three million miles away.

When the snow is falling in tiny grains
At a rapid pace at the beginning
Of March with the temperature around
Freezing I know this is the type of snow

That accumulates and it's removal
Is tricky because it's wet and heavy
On the verge of melting and clogging the
Snow blower so in the evening I

Like to pull the curtains to the windows
And deny the snow is falling for a
While but in the morning I get to it
Before it's soggy and the moment I

Open the door and put my foot into
The snow I can gage the trouble ahead.

There is always
disharmony
with someone
that comes to mind
while I am moving snow.

Galveston — 1900

Galvestonians had no warning of
The hurricane howling and impending
And six thousand were lost on Sunday night
And debris covered the ground three miles long

And two stories high while the bodies of
The missing were swept out to sea but the
Survivors were left with the question of
Staying or abandoning the island

Fleeing the sticky sweltering summers
Saying good riddance to the mosquitoes
And mostly who would abide in a place
Where God had swept with a mighty hand and

Destroyed years of careful habitation
And they decided somehow to rebuild.

Starting over
someplace new
couldn't be done
because their roots
had taken hold.

The Seawall

Logs of yellow pine from Beaumont Texas
Were driven through the sand forty feet down
Into the clay — and concrete composed of
Crushed granite was layered over as a

Foundation reinforced with steel rods — and
Before the seawall was built giant blocks
Of granite from central Texas were placed
On an apron as a buffer from the

Bay — and granite of diverse sizes made
A riprap breakwater extending out
Twenty-seven feet — and a concave wall
Was raised in sections with the curve facing

The water — and a tongue and groove system
Connected pieces allowing movement.

Galvestonians
asserted a wall
seventeen feet tall
above a low tide
against coming storms.

The Galvestonians determined that
Five hundred square blocks of the city had
To be raised seventeen feet so they dug
A canal behind the seawall for the

Dredge boats from Germany and they lifted
Two thousand buildings onto stilts and the
Boats scooped the fill from the bay and by means
Of capacious pipes a mix of water

And sand was pumped into place while the pipes
Were continuously repositioned
And people moved about on hoisted
Boardwalks and by street cars running on rails

That were doggedly reconfigured and
Finally Galvestonians were done.

The engines of the
dredge boats pumped mostly water
but grain by grain of
sand settled in place until
the town was elevated.

St. Patrick's Catholic Church had the panache
Of a European cathedral — a
Stone structure of monumental heft with
A tower and stained glass windows — that had

To be raised so the Galvestonians
Employed one hundred laborers who turned
Seven hundred jackscrews one half inch at
A time and over thirty-five days they

Raised the church five feet and poured a concrete
Foundation and the feat was accomplished
Without cracking the walls while services
Continued without an interruption

Showing that faith and ingenuity
Can in deed move a mountain of limestone.

Not everyone
believed the deed
could be done but
some had to be
optimistic.

Electricity was coming and they
Used steam engines for dredging but they lacked
The accumulated industrial
Might that prepares people today to raise

Towers in the sky so they relied on
Ingenuity determination
And faith in rebuilding Galveston not
So differently from the Egyptians who

Generated the pyramids — and in
1915 a hurricane stronger
Than that of 1900 assaulted
The island and inflicted terrible

Damage but only six people were lost
And the Galvestonians persevered.

It's peculiar
and quite human
to put down roots
on a sand island
exposed to hurricanes.

I choose to believe
irritations are
thorns on the way to
metamorphosis.

Direction and
propulsion are
manageable
while emergence is
unpredictable.

— *Tekkan*

www.ingramcontent.com/pod-product-compliance
Lightning Source LLC
Chambersburg PA
CBHW052102070526
44584CB00017B/2293